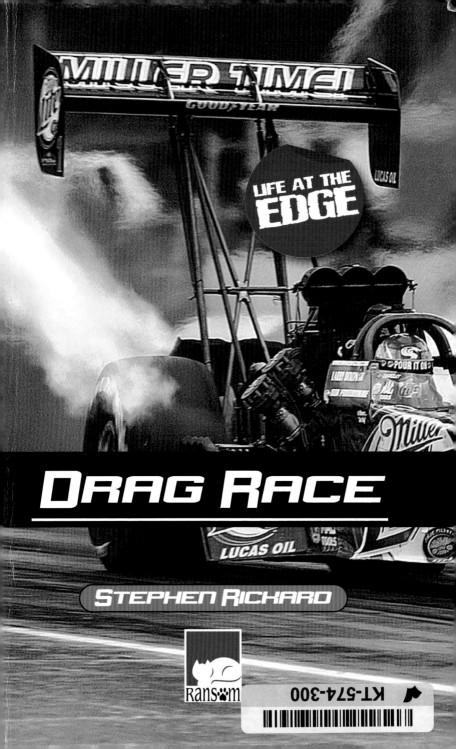

LIFE AT THE
EDGE

DRAG RACE

STEPHEN RICKARD

Ransom

Wings.
Help keep the car on the track.

Fuel.
The car uses a special fuel called nitromethane. The car uses about 56 litres of fuel in a single race.

Front wheels.
All power goes to the back wheels, so the front wheels are very small and light.

Body.
Most of the body is made of carbon fibre. This makes it very light.

Drag Race

by Stephen Rickard

Published by Ransom Publishing Ltd.
51 Southgate Street, Winchester, Hampshire SO23 9EH
www.ransom.co.uk

ISBN   978 184167 759 0

First published in 2010

All photographs copyright © 2009: inside front cover - Kev; title page -
Royalbroil; countdown lights - Sam Sefton. All other photographs copyright
Carter Motorsport, to whom many thanks.

Follow Andy Carter at www.andycarter.net.

A CIP catalogue record of this book is available from the British Library.

The right of Stephen Rickard to be identified as the author of this Work has been
asserted by him in accordance with sections 77 and 78 of the Copyright, Design and
Patents Act 1988.

THE TOP FUEL DRAGSTER

Engine.
7,000 horse power. Seventy times more powerful than a normal car.

Tyres.
The big tyres transfer power to the track. The tyres wear out after about 6 races.

TOP FUEL DRAGSTER DATA

Length:	8.2 metres
Engine:	7,000 horse power
Top speed:	508 km/hour (317 mph)

This is a drag race.

Two cars race each other.

The race is a quarter of a mi[le] (0.4 km). That's not far!

There are no corners. This i[s] a straight line race.

SECONDS

00.00

These are the fastest cars in the world. They are called Top Fuel dragsters.

ACCELERATION

BROWN TROUSERS

Did I say car?

That's not really true.

It's more like a missile with a seat in it.

SECONDS

00.00

My car is filled with special fuel. It's very expensive. It also explodes very easily.

No worries, then.

Everything is checked. Then checked again.

If something goes wrong, I could be killed!

ACCELERATION

BROWN TROUSERS

I wear special clothes. My car might catch fire.

My helmet covers my face. I wear a full body fire suit. It has a fire-proof face mask, socks and gloves.

My helmet is also fixed to my seat.

This is safer. The car goes so fast that I could break my neck.

SECONDS

00.00

First I spin the tyres to warm them up.

This is called the burnout.

SECONDS

00.00

Warm tyres grip the track better, so I can go faster.

The burnout also cleans the tyres. Dirt might slow me down.

ACCELERATION

BROWN TROUSERS

Now I move to the start line.

My front wheels break a light beam. I'm ready to start.

SECONDS

00.00

ACCELERATION

BROWN TROUSERS

The other car lines up at the start as well.

SECONDS

00.00

Watch the lights.

The amber lights are flashing. Get ready.

Focus. Focus.

SECONDS

00.00

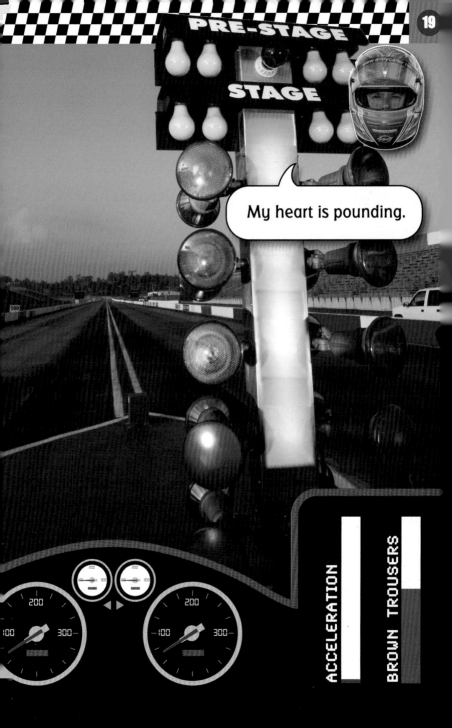

Less than half a second later, the light turns green.

Go! Go! Go!

SECONDS

00.05

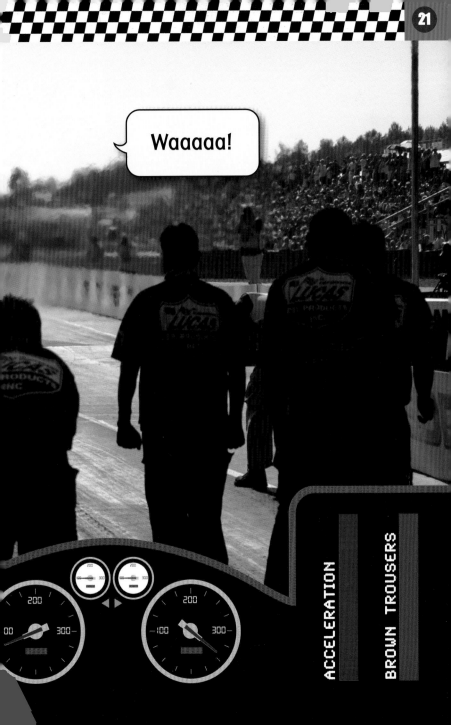

My head slams back into my seat.

The G force presses me back.

It's 6G. That's like six of me sitting on my chest.

SECONDS

00.20

The noise is deafening.

I SAID THE NOISE IS DEAFENING!!

ACCELERATION

BROWN TROUSERS

My front wheels are in the air. This is good.

All the weight presses on the back wheels. So I go faster.

SECONDS

01.00

One second into the race. My speed is 100 miles per hour.

I'm accelerating faster than a jet fighter. Ten times faster than the fastest sports car.

Only the Space Shuttle is this fast.

I can't move. Just hold tight.

ACCELERATION

BROWN TROUSERS

I can see the finish line but I can't move.

I can't hear anything either.

SECONDS

02.60

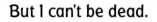

But I can't be dead.

I'm having too much fun!

ACCELERATION

BROWN TROUSERS

I'm doing nearly 300 miles per hour.

Just four seconds after the start.

Not even enough time to be scared!

SECONDS

04.00

ACCELERATION

BROWN TROUSERS

I cross the finish line.

My guided missile is travelling at more than 300 miles per hour.

SECONDS

04.64

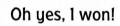

Oh yes, I won!

That was fantastic!

SECONDS

00.00

THE DRIVER

Helmet.
Full face helmet.
Protects face and
neck.

Suit.
Fire-proof.

Gloves.
Fire-proof.

Boots.
Fire-proof.

JARGON BUSTER

accelerating
acceleration
brake horse power
(bhp)
burnout
carbon fibre
Christmas tree
lights

down force
fire-proof
G force
guided missile
nitromethane
Top Fuel dragster